The Spirit of an Activist

Stop Sitting on the Sidelines

By Mokah-Jasmine Johnson

Edited by Andrew Cole

Cover Art by Knowa D. Johnson

DEDICATION

This book is dedicated to my parents Albernice Cousins and Kenneth Cousins and to all my true supporters and allies.

CONTENTS

ACKNOWLEDGEMENTS

First and foremost, I would like to thank my parents Kenneth and Albernice Cousins. If it weren't for them, I wouldn't be the strong woman I am today. Mama when you decided to step out on faith to pursue the American dream, you opened the door to endless opportunities for your children and grandchildren. And papa, thank you for being there for me through thick and thin. I am grateful for my parents and will work hard to carry on their legacy.

I also want to give a special thank you to my soulmate, best friend, business partner, and husband, Knowa D. Johnson for loving me unconditionally and for supporting my endeavors.

Lastly, I want to say "I Love You" to my children and grandchildren. I am proud to be your mother and only wish the best for every one of you. I know I have spent a lot of time being a community servant and know some days you just wanted me to be a regular mom, someone who wasn't trying to take on the world. So thank you for sacrificing your time and for being patient with me. Thank you for allowing me to do my work as an activist and I hope that one day my efforts will create a better future for you and all citizens irrespective of race or social status.

Travarius "4 Pack" Johnson, may you Rest in Peace

Special thanks to Pat Priest, Melissa Link, and Jerilynn Jamieson for taking the time out to proofread this manuscript.

INTRODUCTION: SPIRIT OF AN ACTIVIST

Mokah on the steps of Athens City Hall—fighting against police brutality and discrimination. Photo By Divine Creations.

In 2016 when racial tension grew in downtown Athens, Georgia and throughout the nation, my spirit became unsettled. Racist behavior and discrimination weren't new to me, but it was becoming harder and harder to ignore. And eventually something inside—a subtle voice, what some may call intuition or natural instinct—motivated me to take action.

I was sick and tired of being a spectator and could no longer watch Black and Brown men and women be mistreated, devalued, or brutalized—as if discrimination and racism weren't at the root of the problem. The police shooting and killing of Treyvon Martin (2012) woke me up, but surprisingly, four years later a drink called "Niggarita" made me jump into action. I stopped sitting on the sidelines, and without any experience I entered the world of politics and activism by stepping out on faith.

It was January 2016, and next thing you know I find myself standing on the steps of the Arch at the University of Georgia preparing to protest against bars that use spur-of-the-moment dress codes and other tactics to discriminate against African Americans and other minorities. This experience was my official introduction to activism as we marched in downtown Athens chanting, "Hey Hey, Ho Ho, these racist bars, have got to go!"

"The world will not be destroyed by those who do evil, but by those who watch them without doing anything"
- Albert Einstein

MEMOIR 1: WELCOME TO AMERICA

Mokah at her second oldest brother's wedding as a flower girl.
Photo taken in Jamaica.

In 1982, I was six years when my family migrated from Jamaica to the United States. A few years prior, my mother got a permanent work Visa to travel to the U.S., and with some hesitation, she decided to head for the land of opportunity. A few days before she left, I remember her calling all of us into the living room for a heartfelt conversation. My siblings and I sat in a half-circle on the tiled living room floor as my mother explained that she would be leaving for awhile. My Dad sat next to her quietly. We all had mixed emotions. This was a moment of happiness and sadness all rolled up in one. For many Caribbeans, going to the U.S. to start a new life was like hitting the Jackpot, but the downside for our family was that my mother would have to leave her husband and seven kids behind to make this dream come. And within 3-4 years she accomplished her goals.

My mother worked two jobs, sometimes three to raise enough money to complete the immigration process. During that time she developed high blood pressure and asthma, and the cold weather often made her sick. She made a lot of sacrifices, which included her health to improve our circumstances, but she kept pushing and finally we got approved to come to America.

When the big day arrived for us to take flight, several relatives and neighborhood friends came to wish us farewell. Crowds of people stood

—

in front of the house on a tar paved road, waiting for us to go outside, and we were all dressed as if we were going to church. My dad and two oldest brothers wore a three piece suit, and all the girls wore prim and proper attire. As we entered the white minivan to head to the airport, family and friends cried, hugged us, and shared a few words of endearment.

After a three and half hour flight, we landed in Philadelphia and then traveled to a small town called Reading, Pennsylvania where my journey began as an Afro-Jamaican girl living in America. It was mid-October, below freezing weather, with a few inches of snow on the ground when we arrived. As the youngest out of seven children, I began crying because I was cold and scared due to the drastic change in environments, but once we got through airport clearance and I saw my mother, all my fears disappeared.

It took some time for me to adjust to American culture and make new friends. Quite often I felt like an outsider because I spoke with an accent and dressed like a foreigner, so I never really fit in with the other kids. On many occasions, I would run home from school after being bullied. I was too afraid to defend myself. But on one particular day when a group of kids followed me home from school, my mother made me go back outside to face my worst fears.

With hesitation, I wiped my tears, walked out the door, and stood on the front porch. And "Paige" the chief bully quickly began taunting me to hit her, but when I didn't respond, she walked up and began pushing me around. I was still too afraid to fight back, and some other kid jumped to my defense only to get pounded by her, forcing me to jump into the fight. I hit her while she was on top of the other kid (my defender) but once I made contact, she stopped punching him, slowly turned around, grinned and charged me. The ultimate fight began, and this time, I couldn't run or back down. The kids were cheering on the battle, as the neighbors watched. It felt as if my world was spinning, she pulled all the beads out of my hair and got a few good punches in, but I kept fighting. Unexpectedly, this conflict led to a turning point in my life because I won the fight. I walked away with respect from my peers and shortly after began making lots of new friends. And from that day forward, I wouldn't allow anyone to mistreat or push me around again. I vowed never to be anyone's doormat.

I was no longer an outsider, but once I became accepted by the American crowd, I started to realize that my outlook on life was different from many of my African American friends. As a kid coming from Jamaica, I viewed America as the land of equal opportunity, but my friends (whose parents and grandparents survived the Jim Crow era) saw things very differently. I was too young to understand the unfavorable conditions of Black America truly.

Overall, I grew up surrounded by a diverse group of Caribbean, African American, and white friends. My parents kept me firmly connected to my Jamaican roots and culture. So even though I lived on U.S. soil, it was easy for me to detach from the systemic issues that oppressed the African American community. And I must also admit that I wasn't impacted the same as my peers by racial issues. I didn't suffer the same psychological effects….until that is, we moved to what some people have called the Dirty South.

Mokah and her childhood friends. Reading, PA

Mokah's family and support system.

Northern vs. Southern Living

When I was 13 years old, my parents relocated to Orlando, Florida—the Sunshine state. This was a total culture shock for me because the southern lifestyle was very different from what I became accustomed to. Living up North, I would spend most of my summers in New York, and the Bronx became my utopia. The diversity was refreshing, and I loved seeing break dancers and rap battles on street corners. It didn't matter that I was a weird Jamaican girl because I fit right into the Hip Hop-Caribbean culture. I finally felt a sense of comfort and belonging, but everything changed, once again, when we moved to Central Florida.

In the South, they drove low-riders, listened to chop and screwed music, and kids could care less about watching a good rap battle. In middle and high school, Black and white children segregated themselves from each other by choice. As a consequence, my friendship circle wasn't as diverse. It was as if everyone knew to stay in their place. I could feel the tension.

The first time I recall hearing the words "nigger" and "cracker" was when I entered the southern school system. Fights would break out, mostly in the cafeteria, between the Black and white boys because someone among the crowd chose to use a racial slur. Apparently, it was rednecks against Black Southerners, and neither were welcoming to Northerners— "Yankees" and Caribbean immigrants alike. As a teenager, I almost got jumped by a group of girls on a few occasions only because of cultural differences.

I didn't fully understand why there was so much conflict and friction until I became older and began reading books about slavery and African American History. Through my studies, I discovered that once slavery ended, Florida was one of those Southern states that adopted Jim Crow laws which enforced racial segregation (1896—1965). These laws restricted civil rights and freedom by requiring segregation of Blacks and whites in schools and various public places. Jim Crow laws no longer exist today, but the mentally still lingers, which may have impacted the way my peers interacted with each other during my childhood. The Jim Crow stories also explained why there was an ongoing disconnect between the southern Black and white community.

My mom and dad encouraged me to pursue higher education because they believed that was the key to achieving the American dream. They thought having a degree would help me break free from all racial barriers. Unfortunately, once I earned my B.S., and began pursuing a professional career in corporate America, discrimination increasingly became an obstacle I had to face.

Throwback photo-Mokah and her daughter Daesha. Family Photo.

Surviving as a Single Mom

In addition to having to learn how to navigate through corporate America as a driven Black woman, the cards were stacked against me because I was also a young single mom. By the time I was 17 years old, I had my first child and becoming a teenage mom was another turning point in my life.

During my pregnancy, people would pre-judge and often make inappropriate assumptions. My parents were disappointed, and my dad also treated me differently. Our father and daughter bond was broken, but when it was time for the baby to arrive, he was there for me. Nine months pregnant, sitting on the back porch I felt an urgency as if I had to go to the restroom. So I got up, and soon as I began walking, I felt water running down my leg, so I started walking faster because I thought I was peeing on myself, and shortly after my water broke. I heard a splashing noise as a gush of water hit the tile floor. I panicked and yelled "daddy" and my father came running to my aid. Once he realized I was going into labor, he grabbed my maternity bag and put me in the car. He remained calm as he drove me to the hospital safely. I was in labor for hours. The pain was unbearable. But on January 3rd, 1993 a beautiful baby girl was born.

My high school sweetheart was the father, and we were both young and
dumb. After a three year relationship, we broke up a few weeks before
my high school graduation. Being a teenage mom was difficult, but it
helped me to develop some severe self-discipline. I became a master at
multitasking. I didn't want to be one of those statistics that claim most
teenage moms drop out of school, even fewer attend college and are more
likely to live in poverty. So I worked twice as hard to complete my
senior year of highschool, and three times harder to make it through
college.

The skills I acquired as a young mom helped me to navigate through life
with a sense of purpose. I had to be resilient to overcome the odds, and
through self-determination, I was able to earn a college degree, but I
quickly learned that I would need more than a degree and good job skills
to climb the corporate ladder.

"All progress takes place outside the comfort zone."
- Michael John Bobak

MEMOIR 2: ENTREPRENEURIAL SPIRIT

Throwback photo-In her early 20's, Mokah at a local record store, promoting old-school rap duo Heltah Skeltah-Duck Down Records. Orlando, Fl. This was the first major account Mokah secured as a music promoter.

By the time I was 20 years old, I desperately wanted to FREE myself from all the corporate bureaucracy, primarily because I was tired of being rejected or overlooked in Corporate America. I wanted to try something different, so I stopped conforming to American standards, which emphasize working a traditional nine-to-five job and acquiring material things as a representation of success. To change my circumstances, I began working towards establishing a sustainable business and making a living doing what I love, as opposed to climbing the corporate ladder. Fitting into the so-called status quo was no longer my concern, the goal now was to become my own boss.

In 1999 I launched my first business, a marketing and hip-hop promotions company called Chocolate City Live. Starting this company was the first time I could remember following my intuition. I did not have all the financial resources nor moral support to get this enterprise going, but I couldn't resist pursuing it because that gut feeling told me to jump, so I took a leap of faith. I was young and still had a lot of growing to do, but I was fearless and was willing to take the risk.

Before leaving my traditional nine-to-five job, I began investing a portion of my income into building my promotions company. Throughout this process, I learned the ins and outs of operating a business, which gave me a sense of freedom. I had some financial success and a few failures, and it was difficult for me to build a profitable promotions company. But I kept going. Despite the fact that I was a single young mother, living paycheck to paycheck, I took the risk of becoming a business owner.

Just Jump

Quite often, I hear people say they wish they could start their own business, get involved in their community, but they just don't know how or don't have the time. Well, neither did I. But the only difference between me and many others is that I am a risk taker. I hate to lose, but I am not afraid of failing because I use my mistakes to make me stronger. I don't allow my fear or "the haters" keep me from following my intuition. And even though I may not have all the resources or support, I am willing to follow my intuitive spirit, which has been a critical factor in my success.

So when you get a creative idea or strong desire to do something different, don't allow your fear, procrastination, or negative thoughts stop you from accomplishing your goals. Just talking about your goals is not good enough. You have to take action, and sometimes you just have to "jump!"

"The universe doesn't give you what you ask for with your thoughts—it gives you what you demand with your actions."
- Steve Maraboli, *Life, the Truth, and Being Free*

MEMOIR 3: A CLASSIC LOVE STORY

Mokah and her soulmate Knowa D. Johnson. Photo by Donald Fuller

Within a six- to eight-year period, I had become a serial entrepreneur. And by the time I was 28, I had been married, divorced, and had already opened and closed my second business, which was a performing arts school. I was now a single mom with four kids (three girls and one boy), developing my third company, Higher Level Beauty Salon. I was also still holding onto my hip-hop promotions business.

I became so hyper focused on achieving my business goals that outside of taking care of my children, nothing else mattered. Until, I met my current husband, business partner, and soulmate Knowa D. Johnson. Still, it took awhile for me to recognize that he was the man for me.

On a hot summer day, Knowa entered my beauty salon while promoting one of his upcoming events. This wasn't the first time we crossed paths but we instantly connected, and shortly after our love story began.

Knowa D. Johnson Speaks

The first time I saw her, I was at a showcase she coordinated and hosted in Orlando back in the early 2000s. There was a local hip-hop group with a record in the top five on the underground radio station scheduled to perform, and I was the featured vocalist singing the hook. Most of the attendees were from up north and the eastside of town. Throughout the night I recall seeing this woman wearing an African head wrap with a clipboard walking around all night making sure things were in order, but I didn't get a chance to meet her that evening. Yet her image and demeanor were etched into my memory.

Years went by. Then one day after getting off from work, I got in the car and my then fiancé Leslie Brown, who was also a beautiful spirit, said excitedly, "Baby, you need to get with this girl!" She showed me an article about this young woman named Jasmine who was the only female in the city producing showcases for local artists. Because I am a singer/songwriter, she strongly suggested that I get in touch with her. That moment, like the one before at the showcase, was engraved in my mind. She made an impression, but I didn't attempt to contact her.

Less than a year later, Leslie ascended as the result of a stroke, and her funeral was held on the weekend of our four-year anniversary as a couple. From there I would dive deep into my music and began exploring event production.

A year later while my cousin Roc and I were producing a showcase, I ended up passing out flyers at a salon Mokah owned. Introducing herself as Mokah Dimes, she let me leave some flyers at the shop. She also inquired about press passes to the event because she wanted footage for a DVD magazine she was producing. I remember her having a friendly smile and a warm professional personality. Of course, I gave her press access and would see her at the event, where we would be cordial but too busy to make any real connections. Following that night, during the next few months, I would see her at various events around town and witness the go-getter in her.

One thing led to another. Life landed me in the position of program director at one of the most popular internet radio stations in Florida and some areas across the country. By this time Mokah completed her first DVD magazine, which was distributed on the streets. This copy would become the pilot after she later produced an even more polished version featuring celebrities and local artists. I was producing a radio show called "The 6 O'clock Grind" and wanted to interview her for a segment of the show.

She agreed. I met her at her house with my recorder to conduct the interview. We talked, and while learning more about each other, I also realized we had the same entrepreneurial spirit. She showed me some flyers from past events she had produced, newsletters she started, and articles were written about her work. One article stood out particularly. This was when I realized she was that girl in the article Leslie said I needed to connect with. I also recognized that she was the sister wearing the African head scarf with the clipboard at the showcase years ago on that night. That day I left with the feeling we should somehow work together, but I wasn't sure how.

I liked the newsletter idea she created, and without much thought, I began working on an updated version. The next day I showed up unexpectedly at her salon with a revamped printed copy of the newsletter, and she was both surprised and impressed with the design and turnaround time. I felt good that I spent time on this project, and because of my actions, we began working together.

A short time after, we found ourselves part of a team of individual entrepreneurs and artists traveling and working together to produce events. Several times on the road, we found ourselves sharing a room and in some cases a bed, but there were never any intimate moments or advances from either of us. It was a platonic business relationship, and in my mind, we were sacrificing comfort to save money. These were the times we really got to see each other in action with no sense of trying to impress each other. Every adventure we went on only made me respect her mind even more. A lot of times she would be the only female traveling with us, but her presence demanded respect without ever having to open her mouth. Some of our associates joked periodically about how we should get together, but we both had our own dating lives and didn't see each other in that way.

Right before the real estate crash in Florida, a group of five including Mokah and me decided to start a pirate radio station to promote our brands and events. At first, the station ran smoothly and seemed to be a great idea, but soon some of the staff and partners changed the vibe of everything—almost operating completely opposite of what we initially agreed on. So, I proposed hitting a new market I was familiar with three hours away to promote our services. Mokah was the only one who showed interest and was willing to take this risk, so soon after we made our first of several trips to Ft. Pierce, Florida, unaware of what would unfold.

Ft. Pierce is a small town on the Treasure Coast of Florida I use to visit as a teen. Thelma & Bro Sapp was my favorite auntie and uncle who lived there. On our first visit, the objective was to connect with the local radio personalities, the most popular DJs, and club promoters to establish a rapport. We accomplished all our goals that trip and headed back. The second visit was an overnight trip with a more detailed agenda. By the end of it, we decided what event we would produce, with whom, when and where. We arrived around nine that evening and decided to book our room and get started the next day. This trip felt no different from any in the past, but that would soon change.

Later that night, Mokah developed a discomfort in one of her shoulders and asked for my assistance. We had separate beds, so I went closer to massage her shoulder. When I touched her, it was electrifying. Suddenly we mutually found ourselves engulfed by a breathtaking passion I had never experienced. The energy was so intense that Mokah literally felt faint and had to pause. The whole time some pastor was on TV preaching fiercely in the background. There was a moment when I looked at her and not only felt complete but as if I remembered a vision of what my soulmate would look like when we met. We looked into each other's eyes, and all I could utter was, "I knew you would have dreads." There was no doubt in my mind, body, and soul—finally—that we were destined to be more than just business associates.

The next day we both knew there were some ties back home we had to cut before we could truly move forward with this relationship. But we were committed to doing so. There was nothing we wanted more. Mary J. Blige's song "Seven Days" became our theme song as we traveled back to Orlando to break this incredible news to our family, friends, and business associates.

Later we would experience several twists and turns, ups and downs, on our journey. Our complete story is one of destiny filled with adventure, chance, struggle, and love. Regardless of all the challenges, I wouldn't trade the experience for the world.

Mokah Speaks

Now almost 12 years later we are still together making power moves and loving each other unconditionally.

With Knowa's support, in 2007 I was able to go back to school to pursue my M.S. Degree in Education, Media Design, and Technology at Full Sail University, Winter Park Florida. I was overly excited when I got accepted to attend "Full Sail" because it was one of the only schools in the Southeast that successfully catered to students in the entertainment industry, from film to music. While working on my Masters, Knowa and I continued hosting hip-hop showcases, promoting artists through our popular DVD Magazine, "Chocolate City Live," and building our company brand in Central Florida.

Through the DVD Magazine and showcases, we contributed to the growth of the Central Florida hip-hop music scene. Still yet, we knew, to go to the next level we had to try something different. Around this time, several of our friends and business associates, had relocated to Atlanta and they continuously encouraged us to join them. Eventually, we did.

"Living life with no regrets, I stepped out on faith with my soulmate and never looked back. He was the missing piece to my puzzle."

MEMOIR 4: A NEW BEGINNING

Celebrity rapper Nelly and mega producer Jermaine Dupri.
Photo by Knowa D. Johnson

Welcome to Atlanta

After earning my Master's Degree from Full Sail University in 2009, Knowa and I closed shop, packed up our bags, and relocated to Atlanta with the kids. We only had enough money to pay rent for four months, but we had big dreams of expanding our business. We felt we were outgrowing the Orlando market and believed that moving to Atlanta would be better for us because it had become the new hip-hop mecca.

We were a little skeptical about leaving everything behind, all that was familiar to us. We didn't know what to expect, but when we drove into ATL, listening to v103 radio station and seeing many billboard advertisements featuring Black business owners along the highway, we felt reassured that we made the right move.

Atlanta gave me hope because I was surrounded by my ideal target audience. I was interacting with more Black people in prominent positions from bank managers to club owners (upscale clubs—not some hole in the wall). I also like seeing judges and lawyers (with dreadlocks), Black doctors with their respected practices, mayor to members of

Congress and various Black people of wealth. I felt revitalized and empowered.

Within 24 hours of moving into our new apartment in Norcross, Ga, we hit the ground running. Knowa's childhood friend "Doc" Holmes owned a record label and a new magazine company. He needed help with promoting his new artists, so he invited us to an industry party in Downtown ATL. We decided to join him because this was an efficient way for us to make some connections. He picked us up later that night and went to some Bowling Alley in Duluth, Georgia. This was a celebrity fundraiser for Hosea Feeds the Hungry. I don't remember the name of the venue, but I do remember meeting Nelly and Jermaine Dupri; Khandi Burress, Housewives of Atlanta TV personality and singer; and Frankie, and Neffe-two of Atlanta's original reality TV stars and the sister and mother of famous R&B vocalist Keisha Cole. Knowa and I mixed and mingled throughout the night and got some good contacts. Doc was impressed by how well Knowa and I worked together, and a few days later asked us to join his team.

This new partnership led to me becoming the managing editor for Flyer Promo ATL magazine. My duties entailed securing celebrity interviews, writing press releases, doing online promotions, and selecting content for the magazine. Knowa handled the graphics and was the marketing director. Working with Doc was an excellent way for us to rebuild our contacts and get our feet wet in the ATL market. Over the next few months, we networked with some of Atlanta's key players and veterans in the music industry. And we were able to quickly break into the ATL industry because of our experience and net worth.

I enjoyed the ATL Lifestyle because there were more jobs and business opportunities for Black professionals. Surrounded by educated and driven African Americans in various leadership positions, I did not have to deal with the traditional racial barriers, but the competition was heavy.

After a couple of years of working in ATL music industry, life became daunting, and I wanted to slow down. The music business can be very competitive, and while staying on top of the latest trends and attending various late night events, I became distracted by the more essential things in life. I didn't want to lose myself while trying to achieve my career goals. Moreover, I did not want to get caught up in the fast lane, nor was I interested in "keeping up with the Joneses."

So I began focusing more on family and exploring my career options as a professional educator. I had to remain true to myself and my family, even if that meant letting go of certain things and trying something different. Unexpectedly, a few months later we stumbled across a town called Athens, Georgia.

Small Town Living

Fall 2011: my family and I visited Athens, Georgia, for the first time when my niece Kat relocated from Boston, Massachusetts, after accepting a job offer as a psychologist at a local clinic.

While visiting her, we decided to go downtown to check out the small town. I remember walking down Clayton Street holding hands with my husband and hearing a band practice in a nearby apartment above a local business. The window was open, curtains pulled back, and we could see the drummer inside playing in a dimly lit room. A few blocks down the street on the corner of College Avenue, a street musician was strumming on his guitar for pay. These scenes reminded me of the time I spent in New York City, walking through the subway surrounded by talented musicians and singers, feeling a sense of freedom of expression. We fell in love with this quaint small town less than 90 minutes northeast of Atlanta, which we now call home.

I believe we were drawn to Athens for a higher purpose than we could have ever conceived, and all indications reaffirm that belief over the years. I always loved big city living, but I couldn't resist the creative and cozy Classic City. So we decided to relocate to Athens during the fall of 2011 to raise our children and expand our business.

Athens Hip Hop and the Black Community

Once we found an apartment and got settled on the Westside of Athens, Knowa and I began exploring the hip-hop music scene. We quickly realized that the local music community catered mostly to indie rock and folk bands that continuously overshadowed Athens urban music culture. We also noticed that hip-hop had acquired a bad reputation in the downtown area. Most venues did not openly accept us as promoters and at that time (2011-12), there were no open mics or hip-hop showcases happening in Athens so we began thinking of ways we could stimulate the market.

As we were looking for solutions, my husband stumbled across a newspaper article about a local hip-hop promoter, known as Montu Miller. Knowa contacted Montu, who was very helpful. He knew all about Athens hip-hop scene because he had already put in years of work hosting various showcases helping to keep Athens hip-hop community alive. Montu told us that there were plenty of talented hip-hop artists in Athens, but at the time the scene seemed to stagnate.

We discovered that the lack of support, opportunities, combined with various egos hindered the growth of the Athens hip-hop music scene, which reminded us of the challenges we faced in the Orlando hip-hop community 20 years prior. And we had a few ideas on how we could help improve and re-energize the urban music community.

In March 2012, we launched our grassroots marketing and promotions company—now known as United Group of Artists—and started producing the Athens Hip Hop Awards to place a positive spotlight on hip-hop music scene and culture here. Our goal was to do something beneficial for the Black community, support Athens hip-hop, and let our presence be known as event producers and promoters of this vibrant genre of music. Unexpectedly, however, because we were newcomers, some locals questioned our intentions. We learned a hard lesson about small-town politics and how the Black community sometimes operates.

Thus to break any skepticism, we had to meet with various African American business owners and original Athenians, such as Homer Wilson who currently owns Wilsons Barbershop, a 50 plus year-old Black-owned family business on Hull Street near Washington. In big cities and small towns across the U.S., barbershops or beauty salons have always been productive networking spots.

In visiting most barbershops or salons in the Black community, you will tap into the happenings around town from local gossip to upcoming events. Making an effort to get to know the "who's who" within the local community helped us walk through some doors but we knew only time would bring acceptance.

With over fifteen years in the business, we never experienced this kind of pushback from our community before, from Orlando to Atlanta. Still, we ignored the haters with the help of those few supporters who encouraged us to stay focused on the big picture.

Year after year we had to deal with different dramas. I recall the first year a lady asked me to give her a refund or free drink because the nominee she came to support was not listed on the big screen during the ceremony. I wasn't sure how to respond because I felt she wanted to argue. After running around all day accommodating 100s of nominees, coordinating awards, and producing a show, I had little patience and no time for drama, so I just shook my head and walked away.

 Overall we're glad we persisted because more than 500 guests attended the annual Athens Hip Hop Awards year after year. Now, almost five years later, we are still going strong and will continue to use the Athens Hip Hop Awards as a tool to place a positive spotlight on the African American community and hip-hop culture.

Breaking Point

In between hosting the Athens Hip Hop Award, we worked odd jobs while operating our marketing and event production company. To stay afloat, we also had to continue doing business in ATL even though we disliked the commute. When Knowa's recurring back injury caused him to stop working, things went downhill fast because we were already struggling financially and for several weeks, he couldn't stand upright or sit at a computer to do any graphic design work or promotional jobs for his clients. These chain of events started a downward spiral for us financially. After being out of production for almost a month, it was difficult for us to keep up with the bills.

Even though we lived in Athens for almost three years and tried to invest in the community in different ways, we didn't have any real friends or family whom we could rely on. Regrettably due to the absence of entrepreneurial resources, job opportunities, and lack of family support in Athens, we packed up and left the Classic City during the summer of 2014. We didn't have enough money to move to another apartment, so we headed back to Atlanta where we felt we could get some support.

We wanted to stay close to both Athens and Atlanta, and we also wanted to put the kids into a good school system, so we moved into a hotel in Snellville, Georgia as a temporary solution. We only had enough money to pay for a two-week stay, and the real struggle began. Week after week, we scuffled to pay for our kitchenette. I experienced one of the most challenging times in my life. We were homelessness. Despite the circumstances, we refused to move back to Orlando, and it took several months before we could get back on our feet.

It was tough to save up enough money while living in a hotel, and we didn't know how we were going to overcome this obstacle. I distinctly remember one night on my knees crying out to God, asking "Why me? why is this happening to us?" When that inner voice replied "Why not you? I don't owe you anything." I stopped crying and began thinking about my blessings and not my troubles. God doesn't owe me anything. Hardship is a part of life, and I couldn't let this situation break me.

Then the holidays came around, and the kid's grandparents' purchased tickets so they could visit them in Florida for Christmas. Well, thanks to ATL's unexpected late-night construction and terrible traffic, the kids missed the bus. We were all disappointed. We didn't want the kids to have a bad Christmas, so we took all the money we had to repurchase tickets for them to catch the next bus and off they went to Florida. We exhausted all our funds when we decided to repurchase those bus tickets, and Knowa and I had no idea how we were going to pay for the next couple of nights at the hotel.

The following day, right before checkout, we went to the corner store to get something to eat. As I was leaving the store, I got pulled over by the police and wasn't sure why. I was emotionally drained, and I couldn't deal with getting a ticket or being harassed by the police.

I already had my I.D. and insurance on my lap when the officer walked up to my door. I rolled down the window, and then he asked me, "Have you ever heard of secret Santa?" I looked at him like he was crazy and said no. He replied, "Well, Santa told me to give you this," and he handed me 100 dollars. I was in shock and told him to stop playing. He began to explain that this was Gwinnett County Police Department's way to celebrate the holidays and give back to the community. I started crying, hugged him, and Knowa came out of the car to shake his hand and thank him, too. At that moment, I was reassured that a higher power had our back. I mean it's remarkable when two Black people get pulled over by the police to receive money and not a ticket or get arrested. I don't know how long or if Gwinnett County Police Department continued doing this program, but it was a real blessing for us at that moment.

After the Christmas holidays, the kids came back from Orlando, and we spent approximately five months living in and out of hotels, staying with ATL friends and moving around until January 2015. Surprisingly an

Athenian man named Michael Smith entered our lives. Before we left Athens, Mike was someone we crossed paths with a few times at a local coffee shop called "Jittery Joes." Knowa and Mike formed a unique friendship, and they stayed in touch with each other.

While we were struggling, Mike was one of the few people who checked on us. We are private people, so we never disclosed how detrimental the situation was, but he could sense we were going through a hard time. On more than one occasion, Mike asked us if we planned on moving back to Athens. He kept saying that Athens needed people like us, and he believed in us as a couple and as event producers. Eventually, Mike offered to let us stay at a vacant house he showed us several months before we moved out of Classic City. And after much thought, we took the opportunity to move back.

The house was being renovated, so it was empty, and Mike lived in a cozy apartment on the Westside, with his wife Kelly, daughter, and father in law. This gave us an opportunity to move in without a deposit and they allowed us to live month to month. We still weren't sure if we made the right move, but business started to pick up. Also, we missed the small-town vibe and Jittery Joe's coffee in the morning, so overall I was happy to be back.

When I was a child, my mother would say to me, "What doesn't kill you will only make you stronger," and this experience made me stronger spiritually. Under those circumstances, we kept pushing forward, we never gave up, and within two months of moving back to Athens we hosted the 4th Annual Athens Hip Hop Awards, and a few months later, we became activists and community leaders.

Before that situation, I had never experienced poverty. My parents worked hard to provide a comfortable lifestyle. I grew up having strong family support and getting most of the things I wanted. So it was tough for me to accept my circumstances. I hated the fact that my children had to go through this experience, but they handled it well.

Living in Poverty

Living in poverty can be a crippling experience. I met many good people in bad situations, and each person had a different story about what lead them down the path of homelessness. A sudden loss of income, lack of resources, injuries, medical emergencies, abuse, bad decision-making, and various unforeseen circumstances are among the many reasons why people live in poverty. And it's easy for others to judge and look down on you, especially if they have never been in your position.

In this society we're so busy trying to survive or keep up with the Joneses that we have become desensitized to issues such as homelessness, systemic racism, and abuse. And it's even more difficult for people who have a six-figure income or come from a wealthy background to relate to poor people.

Knowa and I were able to get back on our feet through prayer, sacrifice, and strategy; also because of good people like Mike and his family. When my dark cloud consumed me, I couldn't see the lesson I needed to learn. I didn't think it was fair that I was homeless because we tried to live right and do right, but my perspective became clear after I had that "God Help Me" moment.

I am now thankful that we choose to fight through those difficult times because it changed me. I developed more compassion for others who struggled with breaking free from the chains of poverty. This experience was humbling. Looking back, I now realize it prepared me for a future in activism.

"The adventure of life is to learn."
- William Arthur Ward

Over 500 people attend the first Athens Anti-Discrimination March and Rally January 15, 2016. Photo by unknown photographer

The Rise of the Movement

After relocating back to Athens within the year, I jumped into activism because of a drink? Now, let me explain.

Over the years, my husband and I have heard people complaining about being discriminated against (mostly by bars owners-staff) in the downtown Athens. From personal experience, we have had our fair share of "shade" thrown at us by white club owners because we're hip-hop promoters. Only select establishments in the downtown area, such as Max Canada, The World Famous, Hendershots Lounge, Dirty Birds and Speakeasy (both now closed), would allow us to host events at their venues. Luckily some white business owners liked hip-hop music and didn't care about race. Athens, Georgia has a culture where we would talk about racist behavior and incidents that occurred within the Classic City, but no action would be taken to publicize the problem, much less address it.

When Flagpole, the local newspaper published an article about General Beauregard's, a downtown Athens bar featuring an inappropriate drink on their menu called "niggarita," many residents and college students were outraged. The good news was residents now had proof that a culture of discrimination was within our community, and it was growing.

You can see now why I jumped into action—all over a stupid drink. I watched for a few weeks to see what our local government would do to handle this long-standing incidence of blatant racism in a downtown business. Unfortunately, there was no real action being taken to stop it, and the owners of "General's" continued with business as usual. There was no widespread condemnation or outrage for their actions. I became frustrated with the local system and told my husband that we should do something—*we had to protest.*

I reached out to Commissioner Melissa Link, who referred me to Tim Denson, the past president of Athens for Everyone (A4E). A few years prior, Tim ran for Mayor. I enjoyed watching his campaign. He was not your traditional candidate, who wore a suit and tie and had a cold demeanor. With his bearded face, casual yet professional appearance, Tim seemed to be a down to earth guy who genuinely cared about correcting social injustices. He did not win the 2014 election, but he made a lot of people both Black and white pay attention to local politics.

Tim provided guidance on how to get a permit for the rally and supported our efforts by helping to spread the word through the A4E network. Tim had limited time, but he assisted with the strategic planning stages and made sure I had filled in all the blanks such as securing speakers, getting a bullhorn, to sending out pre-press and post releases in order to sustain continued awareness. He also introduced me to a guy named Jesse who was A4E community coordinator and Briana who were both passionate about politics and resolving community issues. In addition to my husband Knowa D. Johnson, we all became partners in crime to fight for justice.

Athens Anti-Discrimination March and Rally continued

To build a stronger support system, I also contacted the local NAACP Chapter, the Unitarian Universal Fellowship of Athens, several other non-profit organizations, and various community leaders, encouraging them to join us in the fight against discrimination.

The day of the event we didn't know what to expect. I didn't want to disclose that a hip-hop couple was behind coordinating this rally because I feared the backlash from bar owners or, frankly, random people on the sidelines. I also wanted people to focus on the issue at hand, stand together in solidarity against discrimination, and not get distracted by the fact that individuals, rather than a significant organization, were behind organizing this march. Even though Knowa and I were experienced event producers and promoters, coordinating this event wasn't easy. But we put in the work and let the universe handle the rest.

January 18, 2016, on Martin Luther King, Jr. holiday, I was nervous and surprised when more than 500 local citizens and students joined us at the UGA Arch to protest against local bars and business owners, who, by many reports, continued to use discriminatory practices against residents and minority college students—specifically, by enforcing random dress codes or suddenly claiming to be hosting "private parties" as tools to systematically reject patrons of color. I will forever be grateful to those who helped to support and organize this march with us. Our collaborative efforts were an example of teamwork at its finest.

Once the march was over, Tim also suggested that we look into having our local government create a human relations committee similar to one he discovered in Atlanta, which was established to address ongoing issues of discrimination. I thought this was a good idea, and we all began doing research. In the meantime, Knowa and I started working on a project called the "The Beloved Land."

"Freedom is never voluntarily given by the oppressor; it must be demanded by the oppressed."
-Dr. Martin Luther King

MEMOIR 6: THE BELOVED LAND

Smithonia plantation house. Photo by Renee Hodnet

A few months after the Anti-Discrimination March and Rally, Dr. Judith McWillie, professor emerita of the Lamar Dodd School of Art who is an established artist, author, and African American art curator, reached out to us about an event she needed help producing, entitled "The Beloved Land."

As an artist, Judith had an interest in the history of plantations and slavery. She was the first person who brought our attention to the slave remains found on UGA property by construction workers. (More details on page 46.)

She also informed us about a renovated plantation built on a Native American burial ground thirteen miles northeast of Athens, in Oglethorpe County. In the late 1870s, this land was owned by an allegedly man named James Monroe Smith. He was a skillful agriculturer who used convict laborers to maintain his plantation approximately of 1000 acres, which he called "Smithonia." He brought these prisoners from a local jail to work off their time under his supervision, and there is evidence that these workers were possibly "shackled and chained in the damp basement of the barns, while the livestock lived upstairs," according to Anne Connaughton (Oct 22, 2010, *Red and Black Newspaper*, UGA). Many never gained their freedom because they lived, slaved, and died under terrible conditions, and he made millions off of their backs.

Having an event on a slave plantation, where people suffered and died was kind of creepy to me at first. I wasn't sure if people would attend primarily from the Black community because slavery is a sensitive issue within our culture and honoring the dead must be done correctly. Judith believed an event such as "The Beloved" could help her white friends become more empathetic to racial injustices and felt this was also the appropriate way to show respect to our ancestors who lost their lives as slaves and convict laborers.

Judith was the first white woman I met who was so passionate about preserving African American history through visual art and bringing awareness to the injustices and the lives lost to slavery. The main thing I liked about her was that she was a spunky lady, not afraid to call out white privilege and racism. My spirit moved me to get involved in this event, regardless of my skepticism. Planning and executing this event with Judith opened my eyes to a different side of event production, and exposed us to a new group of people "who did not look like us" yet wanted to show respect to our ancestors and improve race relations.

James, the new owner of the Smithonia, welcomed us into his home. He had a very outgoing personality and coincidentally the same first name as the original owner. I don't know much about James's family background, but he seemed to be accustomed to a luxury lifestyle. James was also very passionate about preserving African American Art and wanted to bring awareness to the injustices of slavery and convict leasing. He wanted to show respect to those who suffered and lost their lives at Smithonia. Co-producing "The Beloved" was my first experience working on a production that incorporated art, a libation ceremony, history, poetry, and academia. It was truly an unforgettable experience.

The first segment of the show started outside in the backyard, as the trumpet player, saxophonist, and other musicians walked across the yard, playing abstract sounds as the evening dimmed. Photo by Wayne Kendall Bellamy

Inside Smithonia viewing Purvis Young's paintings with Knowa, James (owner), and Steve Curry. Photo by Judith McWillie

The Beloved Land
By Judith McWillie

The Beloved Land is an event that took place on June 4, 2016, at the historic Smithonia plantation near Athens, GA, where the house and grounds were recently restored by James de Molyneux and Rex Crawford, the new owners of Smithonia. The event used the arts and music to address the dead buried there to give Athens a sense of deep history—one that goes farther back in time than the city's founding and the establishment of UGA.

Now there are no markers or published histories of the native and enslaved dead of the 18th and 19th centuries nor of the buried prisoners who perished during the period of convict leasing after the Civil War. Coincidentally, many bodies were recently discovered on UGA's campus while building a new wing of Baldwin Hall. Others remain interred under UGA's buildings, including the former art building on Jackson St., and they are inaccessible for re-burial.

Steven Scurry, a poet and independent scholar of the First Nation People of Oglethorpe, Clarke, and Oconee Counties, discovered accounts of individuals living and interacting near what later became Smithonia plantation in the period before the current boundaries of Clarke and Oglethorpe Counties were established. The poetry and music of The Beloved Land references these accounts and was composed specifically for the event by Peter Sloan, an improvisational musician and composer (as well as graduate of Mills College).

The ceremony took place at sunset, from 8:00 pm to 9:30 pm on June 4, 2016, and consisted of an orientation by Steven Scurry, music and poetry in three rooms of the plantation house and on the grounds, and an exhibit of paintings by Purvis Young and Judith McWillie. The evening culminated with a libation ceremony that directly addressed the dead, in which both audience and performers encircled a large functional well inside of the main house. They drew water from the well and proceeded outside to pour a libation into a container in the center of the grave site.

The bodies at Smithonia were interred under what is now both the outside and the inside of the main house. Some native graves are over 1000 years old.

We kept our plans for this event confidential because it would have much more impact if it were a surprise to the public. We felt very strongly, however, that young and aware African American voices must be included, such as artists from Athens' hip-hop community and beyond, as well as African American professionals with strong social and political commitments. Among the attendees were Knowa and Mokah Johnson (event producers and activists), and seasoned Athens poets including Life the Griot and Celest Ngeve and Adreana Williams of the duo, African Soul.

Approximately ten months after co-producing "The Beloved Land," the University of Georgia announced they will rebury the slave remains found during construction in Oconee Hill Cemetery. Local citizens from the African American community continue to demand answers.

Mokah and local citizens march and rally to honor the ancestors.
Photo by Megan Baer

Mokah, Fred Smith, Knowa and various local citizens on the steps of City Hall to honor the ancestors. Photo by Megan Baer

May 4, 2017-Respecting Our Ancestors: Baldwin Hall Slave Remains
OP-ED by Mokah-Jasmine Johnson (contributing writer KD)
Published in Athens Banner-Herald

Built in 1938, Baldwin Hall on the campus of the University of Georgia served as a Navy pre-flight school during World War II. It is currently home to the School of Public and International Affairs and the departments of sociology and anthropology in the Franklin College of Arts and Sciences.

The university announced a 10,800-square foot, $8 million expansion in 2014. The project was supposed to be completed in 2016, but a construction crew found a skeleton on-site on Nov. 17, 2015, halting work until the remains could be excavated. In all, researchers found 105 sets of remains. Of those that could be tested, the majority were of African descent, according to the university, likely slaves because the cemetery closed for burial before the Civil War.

And so there are likely slave remains buried beneath the pre-World War II-era building and multimillion-dollar expansion at the corner of Jackson and Baldwin streets, according to Laurie Reitsema, the University of

Georgia assistant professor of anthropology who was tasked with excavation and assessment of the remains first discovered during the November 2015 renovation.

In an interview with NPR's Bradley George, Reitsema said, "Some of them remained unexcavated because they were partially underneath the foundation of the building adjacent the Old Athens or Jackson Street Cemetery. And from the remaining graves that were excavated, 63 of them had some human remains that we could observe and study."

And while the University of Georgia reinterred a set of 105 remains on March 20 at Oconee Hill Cemetery, the Athens African American community to which those likely slave remains belonged had little involvement or input on those plans or with the ceremony, which lasted roughly 15 minutes. In fact, the bodies were reinterred in secret, behind a locked Oconee Hill Cemetery gate.

Therefore, we will stand in the gap. On Thursday, May 4, the Athens Anti-Discrimination Movement and the Athens Area Black History Committee led by Fred Smith will honor our ancestors and finally lay them to rest as part of Day of Jubilee, a celebration commemorating the end of slavery in Athens. It was Thursday, May 4, 1865—what later became known as the "Day of Jubilee"—when Union soldiers arrived in Clarke County and freed the county's roughly 5,000 slaves. These emancipated slaves hoisted an American flag up the flagpole in front of Athens Town Hall and danced in celebration around "the flagpole of liberty."

To commemorate this day of freedom, we will hold a vigil and rally beginning at 5:30 p.m. at the UGA Arch. From there, we will march to the flagpole at Athens City Hall, where we will have a program of celebration with speakers, music, and poetry.

Our goal is to honor the lives of these individuals and their contribution to the Athens we all live in today. Many community leaders believe the

---

bodies should have been buried with their free ancestors in one of Athens' historic African American cemeteries, not in Oconee Hill, with their likely slave masters and their masters' descendants.

Prior to the celebration, a small group of citizens made up of residents and university professionals will lay a memorial wreath at Baldwin Hall. They will take part in an ancient African libation ceremony to honor the deceased who have been disturbed, unearthed, examined, and reinterred, and those who remain there—trapped underneath thousands of pounds of concrete, glass, and steel. We honor and celebrate our ancestors because we must.

The day of the rally and vigil, it rained and the skies thundered for most of the time. I knew the weather would lead to a low turnout, but we did not want to cancel the vigil. Rain or shine, a core group of us was willing to attend the rally.

In spite of the gloomy weather and my concerns, we had a good turnout, and many people attended. By the time we marched to the steps of Athens City Hall, the rain had held up long enough for us to have a successful rally for our ancestors.

"A people without knowledge of their past history origin and culture is like a tree without roots"
- Marcus Garvey

Stop the Killing Vigil and Rally

Athens-Clarke County citizens stand in unity against police brutality.
Photo by Dive Creations.

On July 5, 2016, Alton Sterling of Baton Rouge was shot and killed at close range while being held down on the ground by police officers. Within 24 hours, Philando Castile was shot and killed by a Minnesota police officer during a July 6, 2016, traffic stop with his girlfriend and her four-year-old daughter in the car. I was horrified and deeply affected by these acts. I felt outraged and could see many people on social media felt the same way.

Tim Denson and a few others messaged me on Facebook to see how I felt about these two incidents. I expressed anger, and as a mother felt empathy for the victims' families. He encouraged me to organize a rally to help release some of the negative tension. At first, I was reluctant because of all the anger and frustration that was circulating within the community. I didn't want to cause any friction between local officers and citizens, but I also wanted to send a message that we would not tolerate racial profiling or police brutality in our community.

On July 7th, 2016, five Dallas police officers were killed in the act of vengeance during a peaceful protest over the recent shootings of Philando and Alton. Various news reports stated that Michah Johnson the African American gunman "wanted to kill white people, especially officers," according to Dallas Police officer David Brown-Huffington Post. I did not agree with his murderous actions, but I understood that many people were angry and hurt and wanted all of the killing to stop. Violence also occurred in Georgia, Tennessee, and Missouri. I feared this kind of behavior would lead to a race war and the imposition of martial law. Therefore, I set my fears aside and began organizing the "Stop the Killing Vigil and Rally."

So once again I was driven to jump into activism mode as tensions rose when police shot and killed Philando Castile and Alton Sterlin. We needed to organize this vigil quickly to help our community heal and due to limited time, we didn't have much help with the initial planning and execution. Once the online promotions began, the word quickly got around and Tim, Knowa, Mike and I did the legwork.

Forty-eight hours prior to the event, I was surprised to receive a phone call from one of the Athens-Clarke County Police sergeants. He expressed that the department wanted to help make this event go smoothly. I was pleased to know that they wanted to work with us, not against us and didn't mind having officers nearby just in case things got out of hand but didn't want to agitate the crowd. So we both agreed it would be best to have the officers monitor the rally from a distance and not to wear any military gear.

On a sweltering hot summer day, July 10, 2016, just a few days after the shooting of Philando Castile hundreds of local citizens, peacefully gathered in unity at the steps of Athens City Hall. Some citizens voluntarily brought cases of bottled water to share, in addition bringing flowers for the vigil and signage stating "Black Lives Matter." I felt empowered, as a diverse group of citizens, Black, Brown, and white, stood side by side against police brutality and to show their respect to the men who lost their lives.

Moment of Realization

Surrounded by a crowd of people, with emotions running high, I spoke from the heart. I shared with the audience my fears, stating that on many days "I live in fear because my son could easily get shot and killed by officers simply because of his appearance and skin color." This experience was so real for me because Knowa and I had already lost a son to the streets. I was tired of losing our Black men and boys to gun violence, mass incarceration, or police brutality. I didn't plan on speaking that day, but it was as if I had an out-of-body experience. I was moved to speak, and the crowd was very receptive.

Later that night, during a moment of reflection, I realized that everything I had experienced to date prepared me to lead this movement. I was not expecting to be in this new role as an activist leader, but all the signs signaled that I was headed in the right direction, so I submitted to the spirit within and let it guide me.

Not Guilty

Almost one year later, on June 16, 2017, Philando Castile's murderer was found not guilty. His mother, Valerie Castile, believed that "the city of St. Paul killed her son by letting the murderer go free."

"I was scared and in fear for my life" was the excuse Officer Yanez used, after pulling the trigger, letting loose seven rounds into Castile within 38 seconds after approaching the car. "Mommy don't cry, it will be Ok," the 4 year old girl said after she witnessed Philando Castile shot and killed by Yanez.

Castile made it known that he had a licensed gun in the car but the truth did not set him free. And in the blink of an eye, another Black man was shot dead and killed by those who vowed to protect and serve us.

One more time: Justified by the criminal justice system for taking another man's life, Officer Yanez was found not guilty, leaving behind a mother without a son, a girlfriend without her boyfriend, and an innocent young girl who watched someone she loved get murdered in cold blood and at point blank.

"Injustice anywhere is a threat to justice everywhere."
- Dr. Martin Luther King

MEMOIR 7: PARENTING AND ACTIVISM

In this photo you will see my youngest daughter Daelynn, Knowa and I at Athens Area Immigration Coalition Rally. Photo by Andre Gallant.

So how do I handle being an activist, mother, entrepreneur, and working woman? Well, to beat the odds, during my years as teenage mom, I had to learn how to manage multiple things at once in order to be successful. During that process, I learned how to navigate through life with a sense of confidence and persistence even when I am under pressure.

I don't believe there's one perfect method to parenting. No one parent has all the answers because every child has his or her own unique DNA, individual needs, and talents. No matter how many books I read or youtube videos I watched, some of my best parenting skills were acquired through trial and error. Therefore, keep in mind that practice makes perfect, and you will develop some of your best parenting skills by taking the time to get to know your child's personality.

Fortunately my children are 15 and older, so I have been able to spread my wings. Even so, whenever I choose to do something professionally or personally that may affect my children and husband, I take the time to have an open conversation with them before making my final decision. I also keep them informed and encourage them to get involved. I am that mom you will see with her kids at a meeting or rally, trying to parent while being an activist but if they were younger (12 and under) I do not believe I could be as involved in my community.

They have been a part of my success and failures, and sometimes I worried if my best was good enough. I wonder how they will be impacted as adults by my work as an activist. Watching them grow amazes me, and I LOVE being a mom but I have learned I can only attempt to be a good shepherd.

At an early age, I learned that parenting can be like a stroll in a beautiful park or a roller coaster ride, and sometimes I felt defeated. To this day, prayers, strong family support, and learning how to listen to my instincts enables me to manage it all.

The best advice I can offer is to love your children unconditionally but do set boundaries. As parents, we must learn how to accept the good and bad and try to give them the space they need to evolve as human beings. Ultimately we must keep in mind that children have their own destiny. Our job as parents is to protect, and guide them down the right path in hopes that they tap into their greatness. Time and attention, communication, love, and affection, are all essential elements every child needs.

3 a.m. Phone Call

Knowa and I were in a deep sleep when the phone rang multiple times after 3 a.m. I picked up the phone, and all I heard on the other end were people in the background crying and screaming, and "Baby Nene" (my step-daughter) saying in a trembling voice, "They killed him … Trey is Dead." I was speechless. She asked to speak to her father. My hand was shaking as I woke my husband, and all I could say was "I'm so sorry" as I handed him the phone.

Knowa has always managed his emotions very well, so he handled the news gracefully. He kept his composure. We stayed awake for the rest of the morning. I was so hurt but felt more empathy and pain for Knowa and Tee Tee (Trey's biological mom). Many young Black men turn to the streets to make a living because they do not have equal access to getting a higher education or a better job. And white America seems to forget they contributed to disparities within the Black community. Trey fell victim to the streets but he was a loving son, brother, and good father.

Over the years, Knowa and various family members attempted to redirect Trey and right before this happened, he was trying to change. He recently became a new dad, finally got his apartment, and in less than one year later, at age 19, Trey was taken from us in a violent shooting on April 2, 2012. To this day, his case goes unresolved. We're not sure if the killer was found. Many of his friends and people in the streets spoke highly of Trey and was surprised and saddened by his death.

For me, this was a reminder that you could lose your child in the blink of an eye. Trey's death made me even more protective of my family. I tried to avoid parenting through fear, but it was difficult for me to let go of my worries.

Living in Fear

Whether taken by the streets or by police brutality, the death of young Black men from gun violence was becoming the norm. Before my stepson's death, Treyvon Martin's murder, on February 26, 2012, was the first significant killing of a young Black man that grabbed my attention. I remember watching the trial on TV, and I couldn't believe when I heard the not-guilty verdict. On July 13, 2013, George Zimmerman walked out of the courtroom of the 18th Judicial Circuit in Seminole County, Florida. He was a free man. In my eyes, he got away with murder, and I cried for Treyvon's family. That was the moment I lost hope in the judicial system.

Both of these incidents made me super paranoid. I remember yelling at my son one day because he came home with his hoodie pulled over his head. I chastised him as if he committed a crime because I was scared that he could get shot and killed by the police based on his appearance.

No mother should live in fear of losing her child, but sadly I know many African American mothers who do. The harmful impact of racism, discrimination, and police brutality is a reality for us and must be taken into consideration when you're a parent raising African American children.

Mokah's son and daughter. Photo taken by Knowa D. Johnson

Black Girls and Boys Matter

Raising children can be very difficult, especially when you're an African American mother or father. Why? Because in this society Black boys are often stereotyped as thugs and Black girls are made to believe they're unattractive or unimportant. Children are bombarded day after day with negative images of Black people committing crimes or living in poverty stricken communities. In the news media, and on TV white women are portrayed as being more valuable, educated, and beautiful and Black women are often portrayed as uneducated, angry, hypersexual, or ugly.

As a Black mother, I worry about the traditional parenting stuff in addition protecting my children from being discriminated against, mistreated, or hurt based on their skin color. I also have to figure out ways to empower them and protect them from all the negativity they may experience on a daily basis, leading them to believe that they are inferior, as if being Black is not beautiful, and pushing them farther away from the principle of self-love.

One of the worst things that happened while I was fighting against discrimination was my 16-year-old daughter running away from home. She was homeschooled, and my work as an activist was consuming much of my free time, making it difficult for me to attend to all her needs. Once I became more involved in the community, there was a shift in my personal and professional life. I could see that she was getting tired of the rules, and like a typical 16-year-old, she started to rebel. I saw it coming. But I didn't expect for her to run away from home. I was heartbroken by her actions, but I somewhat understood.

I tried to incorporate some of the old parenting styles with a new approach, such as using "timeouts" as a form of discipline as opposed to spanking, yet I believe my kids would describe me as an overprotective parent. I was only trying to protect them from this harsh world where Black girls and boys are discredited, misrepresented, and mistreated because of how they look, speak, and act.

The criminalization of young Black girls and boys is an ongoing issue in America that must be monitored and addressed on a state and federal level, or the African American community will continuously be systematically destroyed. So yes, I am overprotective because I don't want my children to be arrested, physically hurt, harassed by the police, rejected or blocked out of opportunities just because they're Black.

As an activist, I always made an effort to teach my children their legal rights and how to survive in this world as African American teenagers. Most of the time it's hard for children to relate to the disparities in the black community because they live in a world that simulates freedom. And despite all the preaching, love, and guidance, kids still make mistakes. My primary goal as a mother is to create a safe space for kids and to encourage them to live up to their fullest potential regardless of all the racial barriers. I try to lead by example while helping them navigate through this jungle.

Jada-Jamie-Dae- Mokah's children

Mokah's son HS graduation-2015 from Youth Challenge Academy

A Letter to My Dear Son

My dear son
As a mother, I live in fear every day because people don't see what I see.
I see a handsome, strong, smart young Black man who can be anything he
wants to be.
I know sometimes it's hard for you to believe
because in this society you are not treated equally.

Some ladies may cross the street, clutch their purses,
lock their doors when they see you coming their way.
White men may call you a thug, so quick to judge.
And the police might approach you merely because of your appearance.
They may shoot first and ask questions later.
And I know, under those circumstances,
it's difficult for you to see your greatness.

I know all this hatred has led you to believe that you can gain more love
and respect from your homies but I need you to see that this system wants
you to live a watered-down version of the American Dream (M.O.B.),
ending with death or a life behind bars.
Gang violence, police brutality, mass incarceration has become the norm.

My dear son
God has given you a unique gift, so don't limit your potential.
Don't fall victim to stereotypical perceptions.
You are a handsome, strong, smart young Black man
You can be anything you want to be.
It's time to claim your throne.

**"The basic tenet of black consciousness is that the black man must reject
all value systems that seek to make him a foreigner in the country of his
birth and reduce his basic human dignity."**
- Steve Biko

Local residents packed City Hall. Athens Mayor and Commission passed the anti-discrimination ordinance-Athens Banner Herald cover story.

The Athens-Clarke County Mayor and Commission introduced a resolution that "condemned unlawful discrimination of any kind" in response to various reports of racial bias. This was something they decided to do after the breaking news of the "niggarita drink" and the initial march in Janury 2016. We felt this was a good move on behalf of the local government, but we also believed something more tangible was needed to address the ongoing issue of discrimination. So, we began pushing for a civil rights or human relations committee. Because this problem could not be fixed by solely establishing a resolution or ordinance, we needed more than a piece of paper. To combat or reduce discrimination and work towards creating a more diverse and inclusive in Athens, we needed a true commitment from our local government.

Once we began advocating for a civil rights committee and encouraging citizens to join us in the fight against discrimination, residents from different cultural backgrounds, race, and gender started sharing their stories regarding various incidents of possible discrimination. This included everything from employment issues and local policing to bars rejecting patrons based on stereotypes like gold chains, baggy pants, white T-shirts, etc. Much of what we heard confirmed that discrimination existed beyond the bars downtown.

July 2016

In reaction to complaints of racial discrimination, the Athens-Clarke County Operations Committee reviewed a draft of a proposed anti-discrimination ordinance. This was when we learned that the new anti-discrimination ordinance only addressed the bars, not restaurants or any other businesses. So again in collaboration with members from A4E (a local grassroots organization called Athens for Everyone), the NAACP, the Unitarian Universal Fellowship Church, various community leaders, activists, and residents, we began attending the Mayor and Commission monthly meetings at Athens City Hall.

One by one we went up to the podium to request that the City expand the proposed anti-discrimination ordinance beyond the bars by including restaurants while citizens held signs from their seats to show their support. The mayor and select commissioners did not agree with our perspective regarding the expansion of the ordinance, nor did they feel that there was a real need for a civil rights committee.

If the ordinance passed as is, bar owners would be required to post a visible sign at the entrance stating their dress code policies or whether they were already closed for a private event on that particular night. These establishments would also be required to maintain records of any private event held at their venue for a year. The ordinance would also give Athens-Clarke County the ability to penalize those establishments that violated the ordinance. This would be voted upon at the next Mayor and Commission meeting.

September 2016

Mayor Denson pulled the ordinance from the agenda for the second time, delaying the vote on whether or not an anti-discrimination ordinance would be created. It was getting real, and Mayor Denson made a chess move. I became highly frustrated and felt as if our local government was playing games. I felt this was an attempt to drag out the process and to avoid the issue of adding restaurants to the ordinance. It was time to change strategies. As a team, we decided to advocate for the topic to be put back on the agenda. We also began pushing harder for a civil rights or human relations committee to be established as a part of the anti-discrimination ordinance, especially if the Mayor and Commissioners were going pass it without including restaurants.

October 2016

Tuesday, October 4: once again we marched to City Hall to urge Mayor Denson and the Commission to put this issue back on the agenda. This was one of the most fun and exciting rally-marches we co-organized. We sang songs such "This Little Light of Mine" as we marched from the Arch into City Hall, packing the Mayor and Commission meeting. A few dozen people went up to the podium, leading to over an hour's worth of speeches advocating for a civil rights committee and for the alcohol license ordinance topic to be put back on the agenda.

This was a beautiful moment because once again a diverse group of 200 or more people from different walks of life stood together for a good cause. Reports from the *Red and Black*, UGA's student newspaper, stated: "As they converged on City Hall, their singing could be heard from outside the commission chamber. " Mayor Denson announced she would put the ordinance back on November's agenda as we entered City Hall.

November 2016

On Tuesday, November 1, at the Mayor and Commission meeting, the anti-discrimination ordinance was passed requiring a visible sign outlining a bar's dress code policy or any closure for a private party. This was put in place to stop bar owners from using claims of dress codes or excuses about private parties to discriminate against minority students and local patrons.

Bar owners would be mandated to comply with this new ordinance, or they could be fined or eventually lose their alcohol license. Mayor Nancy Denson also appointed the county manager and county attorney to gather resources for victims of discrimination to be made available no later than the first of July 2017. This assignment also entailed looking into the possible creation of a citizens committee or some mechanism aimed to build a more inclusive Athens.

I was pleased overall with the outcome even though we didn't get everything we wanted. The reality was the ordinance would only include bars, excluding all other businesses. The county manager and attorney would research ways to create a citizens committee and provide their results and recommendations.

Tension at City Hall

So much tension and confusion occured in City hall that day it felt like I was watching a ratchet episode of "Athens and Politics." City Hall was packed beyond capacity. Seats were filled and people stood both inside and outside the room. By the end of the meeting there were two outburst by my affiliates who helped to organize the rally to City Hall. The one outburst I remember the most was when the Commission approved the second draft of the ordinance, the one without public input.

Well, one of our associates stood up in the middle of the aisle, grabbed his man bag, and yelled "enemy of justice" right before running out the the room. This was one of the funniest and most damaging moments because at the time, I remember thinking "if that was a Black man acting like that in City Hall, he would have been arrested." Maybe I was wrong. But where I come from people get approached by cops for lesser acts. I was also surprised to see the Commissioners go back and forth about selected aspects of the ordinance before approving the second revision.

By the end of the meeting many of us were slightly confused and some thought we lost everything we were fighting for. And the reality is, no we did not get a civil rights committee nor did they vote to include the public input amendment, requested by commissioner Melissa Link, as part of the new ordinance. But this was a partial victory. This was the first time any such ordinance was passed in the state of Georgia or any other city. This was also an opportunity for us to hold bar owners accountable for their discriminatory behavior. They could now be fined up to $1,000 or lose their liquor license if they violated this new ordinance, so I wanted to celebrate even though I knew the fight for a civil rights committee wasn't over. We needed to remain optimistic.

MEMOIR 9: POLI-TRICKS AND ACTIVISM COLLIDE

Local Athens residents at Stop the Killing Rally-July 2017. Photo by Divine Creations

After spending several months fighting for a civil rights committee, and as the "Athens Anti-Discrimination Movement" grew, somewhere along the line the original team members and I started to see things differently. I could feel a power struggle within and outside of our core group. A division occurred because some of the original partners still believed that a civil rights committee should be created and controlled by the local government. I did not agree with their perspective because even though the Mayor and Commissioners passed the alcohol anti-discrimination ordinance, they avoided and resisted creating a civil or human rights committee. I was exhausted from the City Hall fights and I did not want to spend another year begging them to do the right thing, especially when a civil rights committee could actually be developed by local citizens and be powerful with the right stakeholders at the table.

I also began to realize that some of the people who became involved with the movement had ulterior motives. During the momentum of the City Hall rallies, people tried to take over or take credit for work that was already done, and some of the traditional "political" movers and shakers attempted to dismiss us. I started feeling uncomfortable in the political arena and my questions and doubts lead me to research online different types of activist approaches. Various blogs and articles placed people who do activism work into four categories below, but not limited to:

- Idealist activists tend to want a perfect and ethical world. Typically, they have nothing material to gain from their beliefs.

- Realist activists are willing to work with trade-offs and come to an agreement.

- Opportunistic activists are those who engage in activism for personal gain. They may be after power, increased visibility, or even money.

- Radical activists have socio-political motives for challenging the system. Some may believe corporations are evil and they do not trust the government to protect the people or the environment from capital interests.

My research helped me to identify different characteristics in the activism and political arena but before moving forward, I decided to step back to reanalyze my thoughts and restrategize.

Reflect and reconstruct

During my moments of reflection, I recall many times when politics, my spirituality, and activism continuously collided. Because when it comes to politics, doing what is humanly right depends on other factors, such as the bottom line or protecting special interests. I was exhausted from months of campaigning and needed to process everything that had happened.

The good thing is that the movement had a large group of supporters. We appreciated the love but I also noticed no matter how much we tried to help others, some people found ways to criticize and incited hate against our efforts. Those people sit on the sidelines. They are quick to judge. They will talk behind your back and smile to your face, but they're not willing to do the work. I did not want to lose focus of the original goal, which was to break the cycle of discrimination in downtown Athens and to build a more inclusive and diverse community—to create a place where Black and Brown people felt welcomed and were treated equally.

I could not get distracted nor allow my ego or other people's negative energy to subdue my spirit. I had to develop tougher skin if I planned on surviving in the world of activism and politics. With this in mind, I vigorously began working towards establishing the Athens Anti-Discrimination Movement as a grassroots nonprofit organization. I wanted to make sure we finished what we started and I felt that we had to try something different.

So even though the fight against discrimination was frustrating, and I wanted to walk away at times, I am happy I stayed on. It was worth the battle because despite all the tension, disagreements, and resistance, I do believe we help to improve race relations within our community and brought awareness to more important issues that needed to be resolved.

Take Control of your Circumstances

It would take several months, possibly more than a year, before Athens's new alcohol anti-discrimination ordinance would go into full effect. There was still no guarantee we would get a civil rights committee.

The goal now was to take control our circumstances and find a faster solution to help victims defend their civil rights. So we decided to launch the "Athens Anti-Discrimination Movement" in-house Civil Rights Council, which was a new group of selected people that would begin helping local citizens by documenting claims of discrimination while monitoring the happenings of the new alcohol anti-discrimination ordinance.

Creating our own in-house civil rights council was our way of empowering the people. This decision made some of the original supporters less supportive, but many others joined the movement because it wasn't a government affiliated entity. Before making the decision to create this entity, I sought outside advice from people who weren't directly involved in the fight for a "civil rights committee" but had years of experience in social justice. And based on copious feedback and advice, we took on the burden of creating a council that would assist in fighting for civil rights.

The objective was to give people a chance to take control of their own circumstances with or without government approval. I wanted to put the power back into the people's hands by creating an "in-house civil rights council" helping citizens to protect their civil rights through education and advocacy. We did not want to stop or relieve the local government from creating a human or civil rights committee. We wanted to work with, not against them. More than anything, we wanted to work for the people.

I Have a Dream for a Diverse & Inclusive Athens
Mokah Speaks
Op-ED published in Flagpole Magazine

We still live in a nation where people are judged by the color of their skin, as well as their economic status—not by the content of their character. Since Dr. Martin Luther King, Jr. delivered his famous speech, "I have a Dream," there have been many setbacks confirming that race relations are still a pressing issue and that the fight for civil rights must continue.

In December 2016, Athens Anti-Discrimination Movement (AADM) established an in-house civil rights council to provide guidance and resources to local citizens who may have experienced discrimination in downtown Athens. After spending several months collecting community input and reviewing issues regarding discrimination claims in Athens-Clarke County, AADM believes that the Mayor and Commission should consider creating an independent citizens committee. This committee would work together with the Athens-Clarke County Unified Government with the purpose of fostering dialogue, reducing the discriminatory behavior, and creating a more diverse and inclusive community in downtown Athens.

In theory, this citizens' committee would act as a separate entity that partners with Athens-Clarke County Government. It would require a member of the Athens-Clarke County Commission and staff to serve as a liaison. The goal of this new public/private partnership would be to help make Athens-Clarke County a better place for ALL people to live, work, and do business.

Discrimination has been a debilitating problem for many people in this community for far too long. To adequately address this issue and ultimately eliminate systemic racism, our local government must lead the way to establish real communication and equitable opportunity for minorities.

This citizens committee would review community input, recommend action, and implement community activities and educational programs aimed to improve human relations and civil rights. Ignoring discriminatory behavior based on an individual's race, color, sex, sexual orientation, gender identity, religion, national origin, citizenship, age, disability, or pregnancy does NOT nor SHOULD NOT reflect the values of Athens-Clarke County. **I Have a Dream for a Diverse & Inclusive Athens**

Food For Thought

As a Black woman growing up in America, I was taught through life experiences not to rely on or trust the government to fix my problems. How can I believe in a system whose jails are disproportionately filled with Black and Brown people? How can I trust this system when police officers are walking away scot-free after shooting unarmed Black men, women, and children?

There are too many instances in history where the local or federal government has let Black people down. My approach to addressing social injustices is 70% self-determination and 30% political pressure. From time to time, this ratio may change based on the issue at hand, but from my perspective: knowledge combined with strategy and self-determination is key to breaking the stronghold of the oppressor.

"You never change things by fighting the existing reality. To change something, build a new model that makes the existing model obsolete."
- Buckminister Fuller

MEMOIR 10: THE ROOT OF THE PROBLEM

Photo by unknown photographer

I was never fond of the political system or process because there is a lot of tension, egos and manipulation involved. Capitalism and racism is at the root of the problem. Politicians can be cynical, and the underprivileged and miseducated are like pawns in a capitalistic society. Some people running for office are more interested in securing votes, and getting elected to obtain power, and less concerned about improving the lives of citizens. They will promise to solve problems but rarely do they fix them. Now don't get me wrong, there are some well-meaning politicians who will put citizens' needs first, but without the support of the people, those needs tend to get neglected.

So even though many of us don't not want to be involved in the political world, it's still important that we all take the time to learn more about the process and never hesitate to exercise our First Amendment rights. We must learn how to identify good politicians and elect those who cannot be bought off. We must elect those brave enough to make tough decisions. I do believe it is our responsibility, as American citizens, to hold our elected officials accountable for their decisions whether through activism or political engagement.

Like many Americans citizens, prior to becoming an activist I avoided politics or paid more attention to what was happening on a federal level, not realizing how much power us citizens had on a state and local level. From the police department, public schools to the driver's licenses bureau, our local government is responsible for overseeing and writing policies that impact our everyday lives. To truly address some of these everyday issues, I had to become more politically involved at the local level.

So for all the newbies to the activism world, such as myself, outside of organizing a protest, here are a few different approaches you can also use to bring awareness to your cause, but you must also be consistent, rally support and you can begin to do this through:

- Online Activism which entails sharing information via social media. This includes posting "newsworthy" information on various social sites (from Facebook to Twitter) helping to bring awareness to social or political injustices. This method is practical for someone who does not belong to an organization, has limited time to volunteer, but still wants to help support a cause or campaign.

- Direct lobbying: This sort of activism tries to influence legislators (our lawmakers) or their staff through conversation or by campaigning. This may include canvassing and phone banking in order to pass or hinder laws that benefit the lobbyist's cause.

- Petitions and letter writing require contacting your government officials and representatives by mail, via phone, or email to educate them, make demands, and get a proper response or indeed results. This strategy can be effective if you can get 1000s of signatures or motivate people to contact the City Manager, your Mayor and Commissioners.

"One of the penalties of for refusing to participate in politics is that you will end up being governed by your inferiors."

- Plato

MEMOIR 11: BREAKING RACIAL BARRIERS

To help push back against discrimination, Athens Downtown business owners displayed a "United Against Discrimination" sticker.

Late one afternoon on a mission to improve my community and race relations, I rallied a team of volunteers so we could disburse "United Against Discrimination" stickers to business owners in downtown Athens. Around 20 people from the community met at a bar/restaurant called the World Famous on Hull Street. I reviewed the plan, passed out the assignments, split up teams of four, and we began visiting various businesses. The sticker campaign was a proactive way for business owners and citizens to stand in solidarity against discrimination without having to wait for the local government to address it. I wanted to tackle this problem head-on.

With much enthusiasm, I entered a crowded restaurant-bar on Clayton Street called Pauley's. This establishment was filled with 99% white preppy college kids. I felt a little uncomfortable as I walked over to bar. I quickly scoped out the venue as I waited a few seconds for one of the bartenders to become available. I then politely asked if I could speak to a manager. He responded by asking "what was this regarding?" I then happily began to tell him about the sticker campaign, and he replied that the manager had already left for the day. I then asked to speak to a supervisor. He responded that no one was available. I then asked for a phone number to contact someone in upper management, and he stated he couldn't give that information out.

I then realized I wasn't welcomed in that establishment, and he did not care about the "United Against Discrimination" sticker campaign. I remember feeling disgusted by his actions and belittled. I looked around the room and then realized I was possibly the Black person in the establishment at the time. I quickly then said "oh, so it's like that uh" and he responded "yes, it is" with a smirk on his face.

We looked at each other eye to eye for a moment, I felt like dragging him across the bar but I knew that wouldn't be the right way to handle this situation, and I probably wasn't strong enough to get away with it. I became anxious and felt heat rush through my body, so I just walked out before that so-called "angry Black woman" jumped out of me…you know, that woman who people love to condemn once she stands up for herself by cursing someone out after being belittled.

I was so upset. I paced back and forth outside for like 5 minutes. By this time Knowa had circled back around to check on me. He could quickly see that I was unhappy and asked me if I was okay. Once I explained what took place between me and the bartender, he wanted to go inside to confront him, but we both knew this would lead to more problems. While trying to make a rational decision, a lady walked outside, talking to this guy. We overheard the conversation that indicated she was a part of the management team, proving that the bartender blatantly lied. Knowa saw this as an opportunity to talk to her about the situation, but I was still anxious, so I remained quiet.

Once she heard how the bartender reacted, she apologized, and explained she was only the office manager. She then tried to lighten the situation by stating that "sometimes those college kids can act like jerks." She then said she would gladly post the sticker and also have a talk with the bartender. One of their chefs was standing outside taking a cigarette break and overheard the conversation. He also got pissed when he heard what happened, and asked me to point out the bartender and also apologized. Sad to say, she never posted the sticker, and when I walked by a few weeks later, the college student was still working there.

I didn't let this incident discourage me. We continued to ask business owners to place a sticker on their door or window to show their support. This label indicated that everyone was welcomed regardless of race, disability, sexual orientation, immigration status, etc.

Approximately 80% of the businesses we visited wanted to display the "United Against Discrimination" sticker. Yet surprisingly among the 20% was a few minority business owners who were reluctant to post the sticker, because they feared losing customers or that a specific group of people would negatively target them. One business owner stated that he didn't want to post a sticker at his place of business because he feared that someone might throw a brick through the window once they closed, causing him to have to pick-up glass off the floor the next morning when he returned. That was a true reality check, because I had to accept that fear may hinder people from uniting with us.

Following company protocol is also another reason to why the sticker would not be posted. Quite a few managers had to check with their corporate office before putting up the sticker. I thought it was strange that they had to check with upper level management before supporting a cause that stands for justice and equality for all, but I respected their decision.

The sticker campaign gave me a opportunity to get to know some of the business owners and the staff they hired to run their business. Most were welcoming and friendly. The few bumps in the road continuously reminded me why the fight for justice and equality must continue. And even though Athens, Georgia seems to be a progressive Southern town, segregation still exists. It's an invisible line that no one crosses, but when you do cross that line, you certainly know it by the way people react.

The Inaugural MLK Day Parade, January 2017

Knowa and I began planning the MLK Day parade in August 2017 shortly after "Stop the Killing Vigil and Rally." During the initial planning stages, we kept everything low key. We feared pushback from the local government mainly because we were in the middle of fighting for a civil rights committee and we had ruffled some feathers along the way. Our goal was to bring our community together and to use this event as way another to break racial barriers in honor of Dr. Martin Luther King Jr.'s legacy.

It took five months of planning and raising capital to cover the necessary cost. This included getting approval from the City's Planning Department regarding available dates and pricing for street closures, contacting the ACCUG Police Department to hire officers to oversee the parade, contacting the Solid Waste Department to arrange pickup/clean up, and so much more. Once we took care of the requirements, secured a budget, and had our paperwork in order, I reached out to Mayor Denson requesting that she sign a proclamation recognizing 2016 MLK Day Parade and Fest as the first and official MLK Day Parade in Athens.

This was when things got peculiar. After one week went by and no answer, my spirit became unsettled, and I began sensing there was some issue. Therefore, I called the Mayor's office to see why it was taking so long for us to receive the proclamation and was led to believe that the delay was due to the holidays.

Suddenly the person at the permit office began questioning our event insurance policy, and things got complicated. If they did not accept our insurance policy, this could hinder us from getting the final permit in our hands. But I wasn't worried because I knew we could meet their requirements. To resolve this issue, we added the City to the insurance policy for our current event production company, "United Group of Artists," and increased the amount to satisfy their concerns. As experienced hip-hop promoters and event producers, we are required to have insurance for many events and were not surprised by their demands. Planning the parade was difficult, but we weren't going to let anything stop us from having this event.

Also, we seemed to get some pushback from the Black community because my husband and I were still considered newcomers. We had to work twice as hard to rally support from both the Black and white community, even if it's for a good cause. At times, I got frustrated because I felt people were focused on the wrong thing, but this comes with the territory of living in a small town. It's something I still have to get used to.

Even though we didn't have at our disposal all the financial resources, workforce, or moral support, we decided to step out on faith. We worked tirelessly throughout 2016 Christmas Holidays to make this parade possible—from raising funds to reaching out to over 100 churches the old fashion way by mailing out letters.

Many people volunteered but only a small group of people consistently showed up for meetings, and about ten volunteers worked the day of the event. We were understaffed and overworked but it was terrific to witness thousands of people filled with joy at Athens' first inaugural MLK Jr. Day Parade. We used our 20-plus years of event planning and marketing experience to execute this parade—and we created magic.

Athens in Harmony Redux-Press Release
November 2016
By Abigail Sherrod
Flagpole Magazine

Following Athens' first-ever Martin Luther King Jr. Holiday Parade and Festival, which kicks off at the corner of Hull Street and Hancock Avenue on Monday, Jan. 16 at 3 p.m., the 40 Watt will host an accompanying concert, dubbed "Athens in Harmony Redux." The event was conceived during a City Hall vigil in July 2016 that was held in response to the Dallas police killings, as well as the police shootings of African Americans Alton Sterling and Philando Castile.

"Athens in Harmony" organizer Pat Priest was at that vigil. "I thought when looking at Mokah [Johnson], 'Now is the time, and these are the people.'" Johnson, the co-founder of the Athens Hip Hop Awards and a leader of the Athens Anti-Discrimination Movement, had helped organize the rally, and Priest thought she and her husband, Knowa, would be perfect candidates to help transform her idea into reality.

To complete the team, Priest brought Athens-Clarke County Police Chief Scott Freeman on board. In a time when so much tension exists between police and the Black community, Freeman's involvement added to the power of the first "Athens in Harmony" event, which took place Oct. 30 at The Foundry. "This community is diverse in every arena," says Freeman, "and diversity should not only be accepted but should be embraced at every level."

At the October concert, musicians of varying cultural backgrounds, races, and genres were paired up for collaborative performances. Priest says it was fun to see what songs artists chose, especially with the genre crossovers involved. Many chose protest songs from the 1960s that still carry meaning today. Most of the songs were also written and initially performed by Black artists, bringing even greater significance to the performances, as the audience was reminded of how much the Black

—

community has contributed to American culture. Johnson says the successful event "reflected a new Athens, a more diverse [Athens]—a community that supports justice and equality."

With the looming inauguration of President-elect Trump, Priest decided to hold another Athens in Harmony event on MLK Day. Ten duos will perform, many of which are returning pairs from the October concert. Priest hopes the event and its timing will allow people of all races, creeds, and lifestyles to come together as one community—to step out of their comfort zones and get to know one another. "I hope the event does more than just bring awareness," says Darrin Ellison, who performs as the rapper Elite the Showstoppa. "I hope it shows unity. I hope it brings clarity. I hope people walk away with a more open-minded outlook on the human race."

In the face of recent hate speech and hate crimes nationwide, Caroline Aiken, Ellison's performance partner at the event, wants to be "the first one to say, 'Not in my name!'" she declares. "That's pretty much why I'm there. That's not gonna happen on my watch. The more that people do that, the better off we'll be."

Themes of love and togetherness drive "Athens in Harmony." Aiken says she loved how diverse the crowd was at the first installment. "When I go to a show, it's normally all Black [or] all white, depending on the performer," she observes.

It is this mixing together that breaks down the barriers of racism and bias, says Freeman, adding, "As a community, we must take appropriate steps to set community norms that no form of discrimination will be tolerated." As artists get to know other artists, and audience members get to know others in attendance, the hope is that this tolerance of discrimination breaks down.

"People are pretty much afraid of the unknown," says Aiken. "The more they understand someone, the less they'll be afraid of them." So, Freeman urges, "Come out and let the music unite."

Note: Even though I was exhausted from working the Martin Luther King Day parade and standing on my feet for over 15 hours, it felt gratifying to witness a diverse group of people dancing, laughing, and singing along with various artists. "Athens in Harmony" part one and two- (the redux) was a success. Both events brought the community together. I could see that our effort to improve race relations was working.

Policing and Race Relations

Chief Freeman and I began building a positive relationship, and I came to realize that not all police officers are bad. Before this point, I stayed away from the police because of infuriating and heart-breaking experiences with racial profiling, which included seeing my loved ones harassed by officers.

Chief Freeman expressed that he cared about the Black community and was willing to work with us to make sure what happened to Sterling, Castile, and so many other Black men wouldn't happen here in Athens. He believed by implementing programs such as community policing, fair and impartial police training, a citizens' academy, and transparency in procedures, he hoped to begin breaking any systematic problems that can lead to unnecessary shooting and killings.

I cannot say that I have gotten past all my trust issues when it comes to interacting with the local police or with police officers in general because I do still believe that Black and Brown people are a target and viewed as criminals, thugs, and the enemy by law enforcement. And when an officer shoots and kills a Black man, there is no real accountability or empathy for the victim.

Mokah interacting with officers at "Stop the Killing" protest-July 2016.
"I was very nervous and afriaid because usually when I see police officers come around it's to arrest someone. This was the second time in my life I got help from the police as opposed to being treated like a criminal."
Photo by Divine Creations

The Cycle of Discrimination

Lately I have been wondering
If the cycle of discrimination can be broken
Or have I been deceived by the American Dream
Of justice and equality

Following a path of lies and illusions
Bamboozled by theories and false solutions
Make America great again was the 2017 theme

The seed of systematic racism is so deeply rooted
It only needs a sprinkle of hate and misguided ego to flourish
Fueled by emotions and blinded by misperceptions
Running to cross the finish line
but making no real progression

Lately I have been wondering
If the cycle of discrimination can be broken
Or have I been deceived by the American Dream
Of justice and equality

Blinded by the color of our skin, competing to win an intangible reward
The cycle of discrimination just continues to evolve
From slavery, to segregation, to institutionalized discrimination
Prejudice and hate, changed faces but it has never been eliminated

**"No matter your social status or how powerful you feel you are, we are all
equal. We all came here by birth and will leave in death."
- Gecko and Fly**

Proactive, outspoken, and bold women. Photo by Donald Fuller

Black and White Conversation

It's time to have a real conversation. Racism and discrimination have been used as a tool to divide and conquer. It has been used as an excuse to kill and destroy. We have been told so many lies that we don't know where the lies stop and the truth begins.

For hundreds of years African Americans have been led to believe that they were inferior to white men and women. And even though slavery ended December 18, 1865—over 153 years ago—the seed that was planted by the oppressors still flourishes today and their descendants continue to reap the benefits while our descendants suffer. Systemic racism has deep, deep roots so deep that racial profiling, police brutality, and Jim Crow mentally have become the American way.

Race may not be real. But I can assure you racism does exist, and the cycle of hate and discrimination will continue unless we face the truth. The truth is white supremacy, power, and money is at the root. The truth is racism and discriminations is not a thing of the past. It is alive and in full effect. And you must decide if you want to be apart of the problem or the solution. What can you do to make a difference?

30 Day-Challenge

The truth is what Dr. Martin Luther King Jr. and various Civil Rights leaders were fighting for did not fully manifest despite the establishment of the 1964 and 1972 Civil Rights Act. Unconsciously many of us are apart of the problem that continues to fuel the cycle of discrimination. It has become natural for us prejudge, measure, hate; divide and conquer— rather than love, unite, and uplift each other. That is why racism and discrimination are still significant issues in the 21st Century.

Therefore, to address racist behaviour and point of views, we must first acknowledge our own personal biases, and be bold enough to take action when bigotry rears its ugly head. We must be vocal and hold others accountable when they act out their prejudices and bring harm to someone.

From personal observation I noticed that someone's upbringing, life experiences, and surroundings dictate their perception and actions around issues of race. The cycle of discrimination then continues due to ignorance and biased thoughts that becomes a reality when acted upon out of fear, superiority, self-preservation, low self-esteem, or lack of compassion for others. In sum, discrimination is learned. It is not innate. You were not born to discriminate. You can work on unlearning and eliminating those bad thoughts and changing your behavior.

So if you want to help break the cycle of discrimination and work towards creating a more diverse and inclusive society, you must be willing to open your heart, open your mind, and change the way you think about race. Besides what do we really gain from discriminating against someone? Who does it benefit? I encourage you to accept this 30-day challenge:

Week 1: Start with the woman or man in the mirror by answering these few questions. How much do you know about American History? Are you comfortable around different races? Do you think racism still exists? What do you really think about Black people? Write down the first few thoughts that popped up in your head and analyze your feelings. Be honest with yourself. If you answered "no" to question 2 and 3 this may be a difficult process.

Week 2: Open your mind and seek the truth. You can start by googling terms such a white colonialism, racial capitalism, or Jim Crow laws. Dig deep to find the truth about American History and research the impact that slavery has had on our society. Seek ways you can be a part of the solution and not the problem.

Week 3: Step outside your comfort zone and take the time learn more about different cultures. A good way to do this is by eating at non-American establishments such as Chinese, Mexican, Indian, or Italian Restaurants. Attend a cultural fest or party, and while you're there get to know someone who is not a part of your traditional circle of friends. Also during this process, you must let go of toxic people in your life who are racist, intolerant, or closed-minded.

Week 4: Host a cultural gathering-party at your home and share what you have learned with your old and new friends and family. Encourage a positive dialogue. This process may take longer than four weeks, but the goal is to do it and repeat the cycle until you are surrounded by a diverse groups of friends. Your biases will no longer affect how you interact with someone of a different race or cultural background.

"To live anywhere in the world today and be against equality because of race or color is like living in Alaska and being against snow."
- William Faulkner

Quick Tips-Protect and Know Your Civil Rights

We all should know by now it's against the law to discriminate. But the act of discrimination is difficult to prove without substantial evidence. Those filled with hate or greed have continuously found different ways to oppress and divide Black, Brown, and white people.

So to ensure that your civil rights are protected, regardless of race, you must be willing to stand up and speak out during times of injustice, be willing to exercise and defend your human and civil rights. This means if you're a victim of discrimination or a witness to it, you must document these incidents, collect evidence, and/or be willing to break your silence and fight back. "The purpose of documentation is to prove discriminatory intent on the part of the business owner or attacker," according to the online resource, The Law Dictionary. The goal is to build a case by collecting evidence of discriminatory behavior.

Do Your Research
Take the time to research laws regarding the Civil Rights Act, evidence collection, and seek advice from a civil rights attorney if you believe you have a case.

The information below was collected from various Civil Rights resources such American Civil Liberties website, which is a great resource by independent organization that help citizens protect their civil rights.

Know your Rights if you are stopped by the police:

- Always remain polite and never physically resist a police officer.
- Get the officer's name and badge number.
- Do not be afraid to file a report with your local police department if you feel your rights have been violated.
- Ask the officer if you are free to go before leaving. Don't be afraid to ask if you're being detained.
- An officer should not hold you without reasonable suspicion that you have broken the law or are about to commit a crime. Under the law, until you ask to leave, your stop is considered voluntary.
- If you are being detained, politely state and repeat that you do not consent to any search or seizure. During this process, be careful because you don't want to invite a charge of resisting arrest.

Know your rights when video recording:

- When at an outdoor public space, you have the right to capture images that are in plain view. That includes pictures and videos of federal buildings, businesses (including airports), and police officers.

- When you are on private property, the property owner sets the rules about taking photographs or video. They can order you off their property or have you arrested for trespassing if you disobey the property owner's request.

- Police officers should not demand that you delete your photographs or video. Police officers may order citizens to stop activities that are indeed interfering with legitimate law enforcement investigation.

- If an officer orders you to stop video recording or to stand back, I recommend you do so. Georgia makes it illegal to record a phone call or in-person conversation-taking place in any private place unless one party to the conversation consents. *See Ga. Code 16-11-62(1), 16-11-66 (Digital media Law Project).*

On more than one occasion, knowing my rights has helped me during traffic stops and various encounters with law enforcement. So I encourage you to do additional research and take the time to learn your rights and responsibility as a U.S. citizen. This may make a difference in your freedom.

Always remember, "Treat each other with love, respect, and take action"

My concept of treating all human beings with "Love, Respect, and Action" can help guide you in the right direction when it comes to reducing discriminatory behavior.

Treat each other with Love
Love is an act of patience, understanding, forgiveness, and nonviolence. So you don't have to be in love with someone to do those things.

Treat each other with Respect
To treat someone with respect means valuing other viewpoints, remaining open to being wrong, and accepting people as they are. You do not have to like someone personally, agree with their beliefs, or lifestyle to show them respect. To fight against racism, we must learn how to disagree and accept each other, including our differences.

Take Action
Get involved in local politics, vote, and lead by example: stand up, speak out against racial or social injustices within your community and unite across ethnic boundaries with poor and working people to build power.

MEMOIR 13: THE BALANCING ACT

The train behind Mokah is in full motion. Photo by Donald Fuller.

As my popularity grew from my work as an activist, my daily schedule became more demanding. I was constantly on the go from being booked for speaking engagements and media interviews to attending city hall and coffee shop meetings, to fighting for different causes—all of this, while being a mother and wife. I became consumed by work and while trying to put food on the table. I was spending an additional 20-plus hours per week planning community events and strategizing our next move.

Knowa became concerned about how much time I was spending on community issues, and neither of us was fond of the political aspect of activism but I was becoming more and more involved in my work. My passion for racial and social justice continuously took away time from my personal and professional life. He urged me to find balance. At the time, I thought he was overly concerned and that I could handle it all just fine. But eventually I became overwhelmed.

March 2017, after the 5th-Annual Athens Hip Hop Awards, I had an opportunity to attend Girls Rock Alliance conference in New Jersey, which was an all-girl, 4-day trip. My home girl Jenn, who is the Executive Director of Girls Rock Athens, invited me to attend. I wasn't sure what to expect because I hadn't gone on a trip without my husband

———

and kids in years. The last time I flew was before 9-11 and I don't like flying because I get motion sickness. But I desperately needed a mini-vacation.

It was March 30th, 2017, 6 am, bright and early in the morning: Jenn, accompanied by two other members of GRA, picked me up and off we went to New Jersey. We drove from Athens to ATL airport, then we flew to Philadelphia and took a shuttle to the campsite in Jersey where the conference was being held. When we arrived we were greeted by affiliate Girls Rock Members. We then picked up our nametags, beauty supplies, and chose a cabin. These cabins were filled with old school style, squeaky bunk beds. I had a hard time sleeping but the great vibes, social justice workshops, and getting three vegan meals per day made up for my lack of sleep. I had time to think clearly without all the typical distractions or expectations.

Still yet, without all my usual obligations, I was the first one up in the morning with the cooks volunteering to clean up, and the last one to fall asleep on most nights. This is when I realized that my husband was right. I was addicted to working and wasn't taking care of myself. This trip was a wakeup call.

Personal Assessment

After the Girls Rock trip, I wanted to make some personal changes because I now knew I was spreading myself too thin. I needed to set aside time for self-care. I gained clarity and was able to recognize that in this lifetime, I was assigned to share my positive energy and uplift others, which is a heavy burden to carry. And if I wanted to continue doing so, I had to make more of an effort to maintain a healthy and balanced lifestyle, which entailed nurturing my mind, body, and soul.

Time for Self-Care

In order to regain balance and avoid losing control, I began working on managing my time better and improving my eating habits. The goal now was to avoid becoming physically and mentally exhausted due to high tension, high emotions, and being overworked by the issues I was fighting for. I enjoy being a community servant but I didn't want to risk my health. It was time to listen to my body.

So I also began journaling again, which gave me the time to reflect and write down my thoughts before going to bed at night. Writing down my day to day experiences helped me to release stress. And taking technology breaks also became apart of my daily routine. I found peace by spending more time outdoors simply by going for nature walks or sitting outside on the porch, watching the interaction of Mother Nature at its finest.

Meditation is an ongoing practice I try to master, too. I am such a busy body that it's hard for me to sit still and let go of my thoughts. What works for me is when I lay back in a recliner chair or just sit still in general. I then try to slow down my breathing, close my eyes, and begin to say to myself, "Thank You," in repetition until I am at ease. When I meditate, my ultimate goal is to clear my mind and become the observer of my thoughts, not the doer.

To avoid activism burnout, I had to also learn how to say no and know when to let go of campaigns. I also had to periodically withdraw from all political and community-based activities to tend to my family or to save my sanity. So to all my fellow activists, parents, and those with a lot of responsibilities: make sure self-care is on top of your priority list before you hit rock bottom.

"Giving yourself some loving attention isn't selfish-it's sensible. If you feel loved and cherished you'll have more love to give to others."
– Penelope Quest

MEMOIR 14: SPIRITUALITY AND ACTIVISM

Photo taken by Knowa D Johnson

While sharing my story, you may notice I often referred to the spirit, intuition, and ego. That's because throughout my life journey, I relied on my intuition for guidance. As a result, I have been able to overcome some of the most difficult times in my life and achieve great things. I know some people don't believe in God but I do. Therefore I try to be obedient to my spirit.

I also understand this fight isn't about me, but when you're in the midst of advocating for justice and equality, your ego may naturally arise to protect you and you have to be careful and not let your ego control you. It can be hard to stay calm or neutral sometimes because politics can make you angry, frustrated. You can get so tired of all the mind games that you want to quit or literally slap someone. Violence is never the solution, however.

I don't want to lose "my religion" while fighting for justice, so I work hard to keep a balance between spirituality, politics, and activism while stepping out on faith to confront racism. I know I don't have all the answers nor the solutions. I only want to do what's right for the people, especially those who are suffering at the hands of our earthly oppressors. In order to clarify my point of view, then, when I refer to the intuition, spirit, and ego, I mean the following:

Intuition
Your intuition is that subtle voice you may hear right before a flow of thoughts comes into your mind. It is that internal voice, a gut feeling, which can protect you and provide guidance. All you have to do is listen. Often, however, we tend to ignore that feeling because we're so distracted by our surroundings.

Spirit
The spirit is your soul, your co-pilot, the emotion that moves you. I also like to describe the spirit as that Godly energy, covered by your physical being. You must be in tune with your body to be able to use your spiritual compass and know which direction to go.

Ego
The ego reacts to the outside world and thus dwells between the spiritual and physical environment. The ego relates to self-esteem or feelings of self-importance. The ego is needed because it is your mental defense system, but you can not allow your ego to override your spirit.

I truly believe that God has given us all a unique gift, a talent, or a skill you can use to make a positive impact in your personal life or community. But it's your job to identify, cultivate, and learn how to use that gift to change lives, including yours. So take the time to analyze what you're naturally good at and then focus on your strengths, not your weaknesses. There is so much more that you can do and be than what the system tells you.

"The Spirit is a divine, inspiring influence."
~unknown

FINAL THOUGHT

It's not about skin color. I connect with people based on their hearts and mind.
Photo by Donald Fuller.

Discrimination is a sensitive issue for me, because I know what it feels like to be judged, victimized, and treated differently as a result of someone else's ignorant beliefs. And I don't want my children, grandchildren, or anyone to get rejected, killed, harmed, or overlooked on the account of racism. I have love for all people and hope that one day racism will no longer be an issue. But until then, I will continue to fight for justice and equality.

So if you want to join me in this fight and make a difference in your community or change your circumstances, stop sitting on the sidelines, stop making excuses. You got to get involved. You can not remain silent or let you fears overcome you. I had to be resilient, be willing to submit to my spirit and intuition, and step out on faith in order to tap into my greatness. By learning how to embrace both my success and failures, I was able to use the good and bad experiences to fine-tune my skills as an activist and educator.

I also want to emphasize that TIME is more valuable than money. It is one of the most precious gifts in life, so you must be wise regarding how you spend your time and who you spend your time with, because you can never get it back. You can't rewind the hands of time.

So I hope by sharing my personal life story, tragedy, and triumphs that you will be inspired to get involved in your community and attempt to live life to the fullest. I believe you can change your circumstances through faith and perseverance.

Don't be afraid to stand up and fight for what you believe in.

CLOSING

I am Pro Black

What does it mean to be Pro Black?
Being Pro Black means
I love the skin I'm in.
I love this melanin.
I love my nappy hair.
I love my full lips
and high cheekbones.

What does it mean to be Pro Black?
Being Pro Black means
I will uplift Black people
I will not mistreat, or compete.
I will empower my race.
I will seek equal opportunity.
I will exercise my rights and not take flight.

What does it mean to be Pro Black?
Being Pro Black means you inspire others
Uplift your brothers
Encourage your sisters
And show much respect to all the Black Mamas.

Being Pro Black doesn't mean I think my race is superior.
It simply means, I love the way God made me.

About the Author

Mokah-Jasmine Johnson is an educator; prominent civil rights activist; music, media, and marketing entrepreneur; and mother. Mokah is co-founder and president of the Athens Anti-Discrimination Movement, a grassroots organization that aims to combat discrimination through education and activism. **She** holds an M.S. in Education, Media Design, and Technology from Full Sail University and a B.S. in Marketing Management. As an educator, entrepreneur, and civil rights activist, Mokah aims to uplift and inspire others.

To book Mokah for a speaking engagement, for regular updates, upcoming, new products, appearances, or workshops visit **www.mokahjohnsonedu.com**.

#nomore sitting on the sidelines
I pledge to take action.

CPSIA information can be obtained at www.ICGtesting.com
Printed in the USA
LVIW01n1339040418
572275LV00001B/8